Odysseus and the Giants

Tales from the Odyssey

Written by I. M. Richardson
Illustrated by Hal Frenck

Troll Associates

Library of Congress Cataloging in Publication Data

Richardson, I. M.
 Odysseus and the giants.

 (Tales from the Odyssey / adapted by I. M. Richardson; bk. 3)
 Summary: Odysseus relates to his listeners his fleet's experiences on the Island of the Winds and with the man-eating Giants.
 [1. Mythology, Greek] I. Frenck, Hal, ill.
II. Homer. Odyssey. III. Title. IV. Series: Richardson, I. M. Tales from the Odyssey; bk. 3.
PZ8.1.R396Tal 1984 bk. 3 292'.13s [292'.13] 83-14233
ISBN 0-8167-0009-5 (lib. bdg.)
ISBN 0-8167-0010-9 (pbk.)

Copyright © 1984 by Troll Associates, Mahwah, New Jersey

All rights reserved. No part of this book may be used or reproduced in any manner whatsoever without written permission from the publisher.
Printed in the United States of America.
10 9 8 7 6 5 4 3 2 1

"Tell us more!" said the king and queen. Their guest of honor had told of mighty battles and stormy seas, of fleeing from the Lotus-Eaters and blinding the one-eyed Cyclops. "Tell us everything that has happened to you on your long journey home."

Their guest was Odysseus, King of Ithaca. Nearly ten years had passed since he had won the Trojan War, and still he had not reached home. Tomorrow, the rulers of this island kingdom would send him home on their fleetest ship. Now they wanted to hear all of his adventures. "Tell us more," they repeated.

"After I blinded the Cyclops," continued Odysseus, "my men and I escaped. We again set our course for Ithaca. Before long, we came to the Island of the Winds. It is a magnificent floating island. A huge brass wall surrounds it, protecting the people who live there.

"Their ruler was King Aeolus, a friend of the gods. Zeus had made him keeper and protector of the winds that blow across the seas. Aeolus controlled them all—the gentle breezes, the favorable winds, and even the violent storms that threaten the lives of sailors.

"We went ashore and entered the city. The king was a gracious host, and he made us more comfortable than we had been in years. He was eager to hear about the Trojan War, and what had happened to our fleet after leaving Troy.

"We stayed on the Island of the Winds for an entire month, feasting and resting from our adventures. Finally, it was time for us to continue our homeward journey. King Aeolus said he would do everything he could to make our voyage swift and trouble-free.

"He gave me a leather bag that was tightly tied with silver wire. Then he took me aside and explained that the bag contained all the winds that could bring us trouble on our voyage home. But the favorable west wind was not in the bag, so it was free to blow our ships directly to our destination.

"We boarded our ships and left the Island of the Winds behind us. For nine days and nine nights, we sailed across the seas. There were no storms to trouble us, for they were safely locked inside the leather bag. I stayed awake the entire time, keeping the ship on course myself.

"On the tenth day, we drew near our destination. In the distance, I could see the shores of Ithaca. But my eyes would not stay open any longer. At last, I allowed one of my men to steer the ship. Exhausted, I fell into a deep sleep.

"While I slept, my men began to argue about what was in the leather bag. Since it had been given to me by a king, they reasoned, it must contain something valuable. 'Gold!' said one of the men. 'It must contain coins made out of solid gold.'

"'No,' said another. 'The bag is tied with silver, so it must be filled with pieces of silver.' Still another said, 'You are both wrong. The bag is filled with precious jewels. Why else would Odysseus guard it so closely? Surely he fears we will claim our rightful share of this treasure!'

"Then they untied the silver wire and opened the bag. The winds raced out, gusting and swirling in a mighty storm that blew our ships far out to sea. My men moaned and tore their hair as they saw the shoreline of our homeland fade away. We had come so close, and now we were being driven farther and farther away.

"The noise of the storm awakened me, and I knew at once what had happened. I threw the empty bag into the sea and thought about throwing myself in after it. But instead, I turned to face the raging winds, and wondered what the gods might have in store for us next.

"When the storm finally let up, I saw that we were back at the Island of the Winds. We went ashore and took on water. As my men ate their meal on the beach, I returned to the home of King Aeolus. I found him feasting in his great dining hall.

"'What brings you back so soon, Odysseus?' he asked. 'Didn't I do everything I could to ensure your safe voyage home?' In response, I told him what had happened, and asked for his help once again. But this time, he refused. 'You must be an enemy of the gods,' he said. 'I can do nothing for you now. You must leave this place at once.'

"So, for the second time, we left the Island of the Winds. But this time, there was no favorable wind to take us back to Ithaca. There were no winds at all, and my men had to lean into their oars. For six days and six nights, they rowed across the sea, until their spirit was gone completely.

"The days grew longer, and the nights grew shorter. Finally, we spotted land. It seemed to rise out of the sea like a mighty fortress in the distance. After our long days at sea, it was a welcome sight indeed. Now I wish that we had never stopped there at all.

"I did not know it then, but we had reached a land where giants lived. In this land, the days were so long that the pastures were used in shifts. When the first flocks of sheep had eaten their fill, they were driven home, and another flock was brought out to pasture. But the giant herdsmen who lived here preferred human flesh to mutton!

"We discovered a fine harbor that was protected on three sides by towering cliffs. The mouth of this harbor was so narrow that our ships had to enter one at a time. My ship, however, remained outside. Instead of dropping anchor in the deep water, I tied a mooring line to the jagged rocks.

"I climbed up the rocks to see if I could get a closer look at this mysterious land. From the top of the cliff, I could see our ships resting in the harbor far below. The rolling countryside lay beyond. I saw no farms or cities. But off in the distance, a plume of smoke rose into the sky.

"I wondered what kind of people lived there, so I sent three men to find out. They started down a dirt road that led toward the rising column of smoke. Soon they came upon a girl who was drawing water from a stream. When she stood up, she towered above the awe-struck sailors.

"'Who rules this strange land?' they asked. 'And is he friendly or war-like?' The girl replied, 'My father is the king, and he is always glad to have visitors. You will find him in the village at the end of the road. Ours is the largest house.'

"As they approached the king's dwelling place, my men saw that the door was as tall as the mast of a ship. Suddenly, it was flung open by a woman who was as big as a mountain, and more ugly than a Cyclops! She sent someone to fetch her husband.

"The king came at once, and he was even more monstrous than his wife. Indeed, he was glad to have visitors—he reached down and seized one of them, then began preparing the poor fellow for supper! The other two quickly ducked out of sight, and somehow managed to make their escape.

"But the giant sounded an alarm that brought his countrymen out of their homes by the dozens. They rushed about, searching everywhere for the missing intruders. Meanwhile, my men had made it back to the ship and were telling us their horrible tale. I signaled the other ships of our fleet to leave the harbor at once.

"At that very moment, the giants appeared at the edge of the cliffs. Looking down, they saw our ships clustered together in the harbor, and they roared in anger. Then they raised enormous boulders over their heads and hurled them down at the fleet. The huge rocks splintered the wooden ships and sent the men splashing into the water.

"Then the murderous giants waded out into the water, carrying long poles with sharpened ends. They began spearing my men like so many frightened fish. It was too terrible to watch. When they had caught them all, they took them back to their village, where they ate them for supper.

"My ship alone was saved, because it had been tied outside the harbor. I took out my sword and cut through the mooring lines. Then I urged my crew to lean into their oars, unless they wanted to become the giants' dessert.

"Each man rowed furiously, and soon we began to move. As the ship slipped away from the high cliffs of jagged rocks, I looked into the narrow entrance. Inside lay the wreckage of my fleet—a gruesome monument to our fallen companions.

"Then my men hoisted the sails," concluded Odysseus, "and the wind filled them. Our course was set for the shores of Ithaca, and soon we were making good speed. We had lost the rest of our ships, but at last we were headed home."